Saving money made easier and enjoyable with this awesome savings challenge bundle that will help keep you motivated on your saving journey. Use this collection of Money Saving Challenge trackers to help you save for those unexpected expenses and make the savings a habit in life.

Depending on the challenge, choose any amount and save it for a particular week or day. Once you have that amount saved, simply color in the icon on each savings challenge and see your progress!
Start your savings journey!

This awesome challenges bundle will help to Keep track of the progress as you crush your money-saving goals!

There are various interesting Challenges designed to make your saving journey fun and enjoyable. You can navigate the challenges through their time duration, total Saving amount or per saving amount. Following are the awesome saving challenges included.

30 Days Money Saving Challenges
◘ $100 Saving Challenge - 2 Challenges
◘ $500 Saving Challenge - 2 Challenges
◘ $1000 Saving Challenge -2 Challenges
◘ No Spend Month Challenge -2 Challenges
◘ Set your own challenge for 30 days -4 Challenges

50 Days Money Saving Challenges
◘ $1 Savings Challenge (Save $50) - 2 Challenges
◘ $2 Savings Challenge (Save $100) - 2 Challenges
◘ $3 Savings Challenge (Save $150) - 2 Challenges
◘ $4 Savings Challenge (Save $200) - 2 Challenges
◘ $5 Savings Challenge (Save $250) - 2 Challenges
◘ $10 Savings Challenge (Save $500) - 2 Challenges
◘ $15 Savings Challenge (Save $750) - 2 Challenges
◘ $20 Savings Challenge (Save $1,000) - 2 Challenges
◘ $25 Savings Challenge (Save $1,250) - 2 Challenges
◘ $30 Savings Challenge (Save $1,500) - 2 Challenges
◘ $40 Savings Challenge (Save $2,000) - 2 Challenges
◘ $50 Savings Challenge (Save $2,500) - 2 Challenges
◘ Set your own challenge - 4 Challenges

100 Days Money Saving Challenges
- $500 Saving Challenge - 2 Challenges
- $1000 Saving Challenge - 2 Challenges
- $5000 Savings Challenge - 2 Challenges
- Set your own challenge - 4 Challenges

26 Weeks Money Saving Challenges
- +$ 1 Forward Saving Challenge (Save $351) - 2 Challenges
- -$ 1 Backward Saving Challenge (Save $351) - 2 Challenges
- +$ 2 Forward Savings Challenge (Save $702) - 2 Challenges
- -$ 2 Backward Savings Challenge (Save $702) - 2 Challenges
- $2000 Saving Challenge - 2 Challenges
- $2500 Savings Challenge - 2 Challenges
- $3000 Savings Challenge - 2 Challenges
- $5000 Savings Challenge - 2 Challenges
- $10000 Savings Challenge - 2 Challenges
- $15000 Savings Challenge - 2 Challenges
- Set your own challenge - 4 Challenges

52 Weeks Money Saving Challenges
- +$ 1 Forward Saving Challenge (Save $ 1,378) - 2 Challenges
- -$ 1 Backward Saving Challenge (Save $ 1,378) - 2 Challenges
- +$ 2 Forward Savings Challenge (Save $2756) - 2 Challenges
- -$ 2 Backward Savings Challenge (Save $2756) - 2 Challenges
- $2000 Saving Challenge - 2 Challenges
- $2500 Savings Challenge - 2 Challenges
- $3000 Savings Challenge - 2 Challenges
- $5000 Savings Challenge - 2 Challenges
- $6000 Savings Challenge - 2 Challenges
- $10000 Savings Challenge - 2 Challenges
- $15000 Savings Challenge - 2 Challenges
- $20000 Savings Challenge - 2 Challenges
- Set your own challenge - 2 Challenges

Aurora Publishing is passionate in designing and
creating Logbooks, Record books, Journals with
unique and effective designs to bring you that extra
awesomeness you always wished for

30 Day Money Saving Challenges

- ◘ $100 Saving Challenge - 2 Challenges
- ◘ $500 Saving Challenge - 2 Challenges
- ◘ $1000 Saving Challenge -2 Challenges
- ◘ No Spend Month Challenge -2 Challenges*
- ◘ Set your own challenge for 30 days -4 Challenges*

* No Spend Month Challenge
A period of time when you commit to not spending money on non-essentials

* Set your own challenge for 30 days
During this challenge you can save any amount or commit to any saving related activity. Depending on the challenge you decide to go forward, simply color in the icons accordingly.

Each challenge has a starting point and a finishing point. However, only in some challenges, you need to follow a specific path, and in others you can choose your own path to reach the finishing point. Once you start a challenge, keep going, do not break, and always try to finish within the given time period.

Per day/week saving amount is the same for some challenges and it is different for other challenges. So, depending on the challenge, choose the amount and save it for a particular week or day. Once you have that amount saved, simply color in the icon on each savings challenge and see your progress!

Happy Saving Journey !

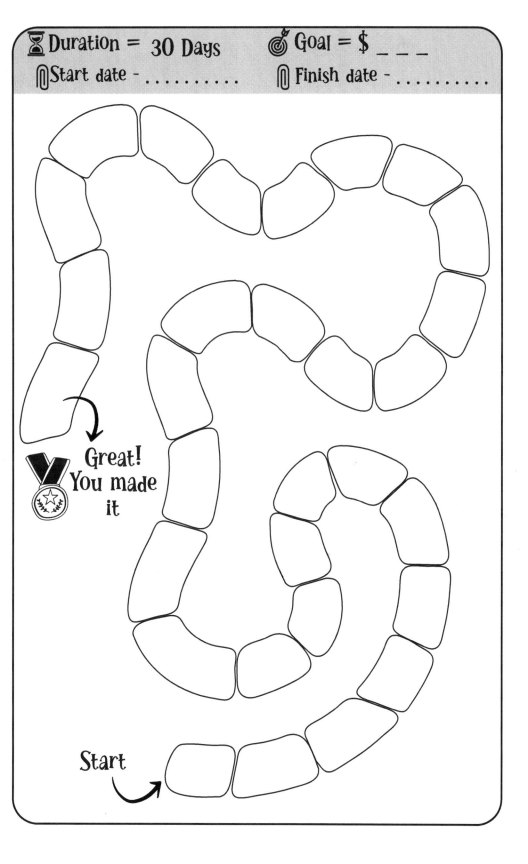

50 Day Money Saving Challenges

- $1 Savings Challenge (Save $50) - 2 Challenges
- $2 Savings Challenge (Save $100) - 2 Challenges
- $3 Savings Challenge (Save $150) - 2 Challenges
- $4 Savings Challenge (Save $200) - 2 Challenges
- $5 Savings Challenge (Save $250) - 2 Challenges
- $10 Savings Challenge (Save $500) - 2 Challenges
- $15 Savings Challenge (Save $750) - 2 Challenges
- $20 Savings Challenge (Save $1,000) - 2 Challenges
- $25 Savings Challenge (Save $1,250) - 2 Challenges
- $30 Savings Challenge (Save $1,500) - 2 Challenges
- $40 Savings Challenge (Save $2,000) - 2 Challenges
- $50 Savings Challenge (Save $2,500) - 2 Challenges
- Set your own challenge - 4 Challenges*

* Set your own challenge for 50 days
During this challenge you can save any amount or commit to any saving related activity. Depending on the challenge you decide to go forward, simply color in the icons accordingly.

Each challenge has a starting point and a finishing point. However, only in some challenges, you need to follow a specific path, and in others you can choose your own path to reach the finishing point. Once you start a challenge, keep going, do not break, and always try to finish within the given time period.

Per day/week saving amount is the same for some challenges and it is different for other challenges. So, depending on the challenge, choose the amount and save it for a particular week or day. Once you have that amount saved, simply color in the icon on each savings challenge and see your progress!

Happy Saving Journey !

50-Day Savings Challenges

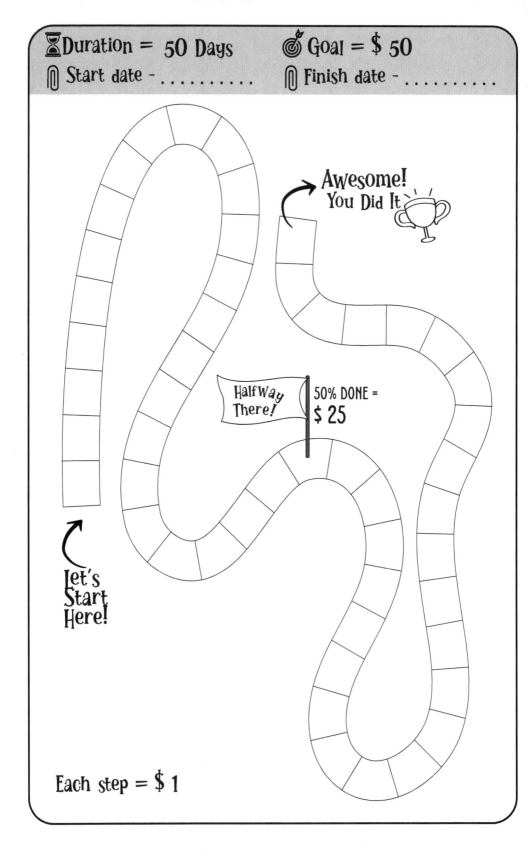

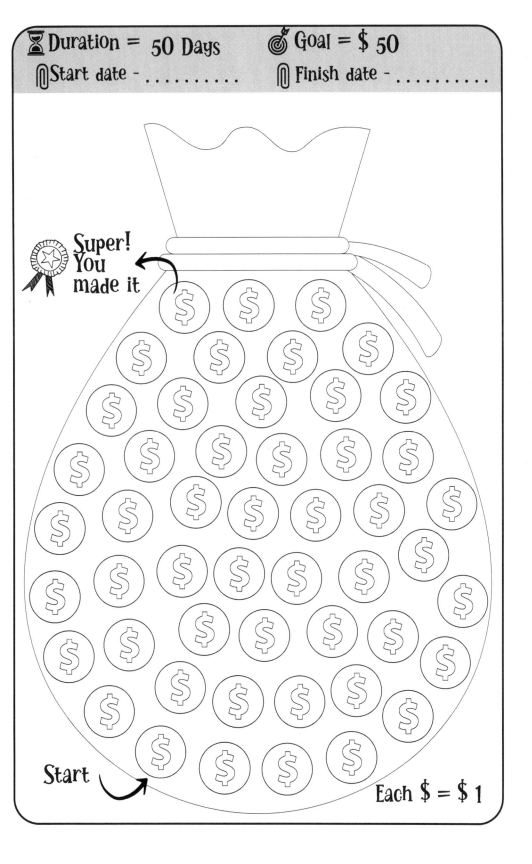

Great! You made it

Start

Each Bell = $ 3

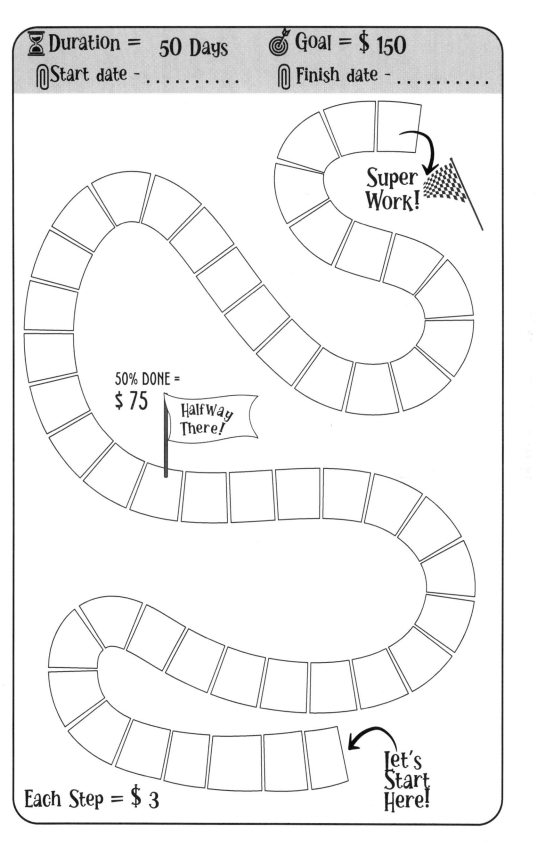

Duration = 50 Days Goal = $ 150

Start date - . . . . Finish date - . . . .

Super Work!

50% DONE = $ 75

Halfway There!

Let's Start Here!

Each Step = $ 3

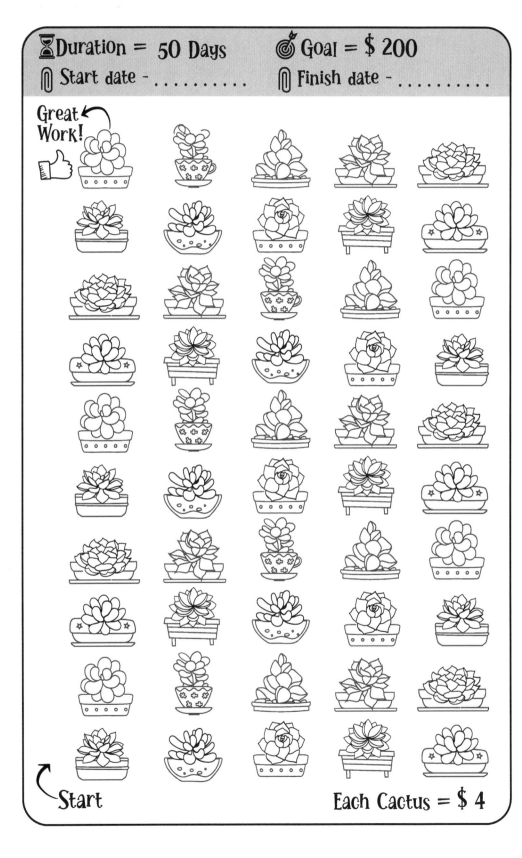

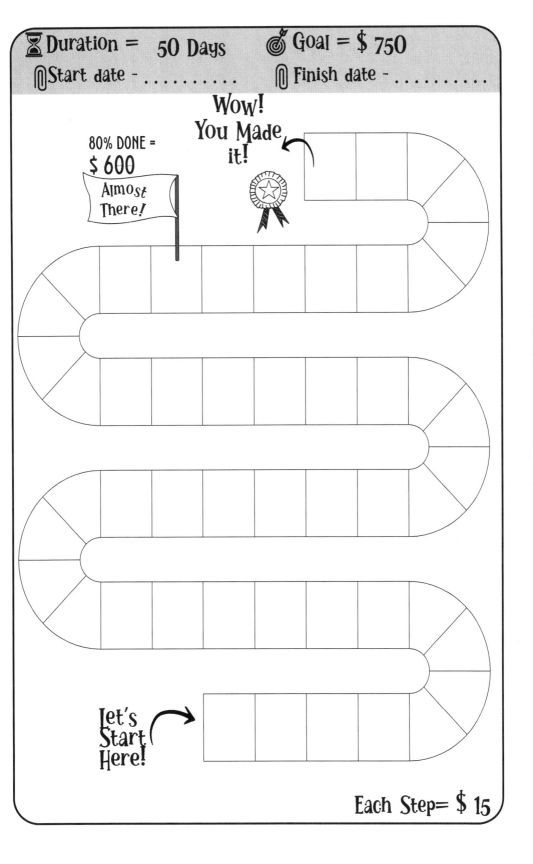

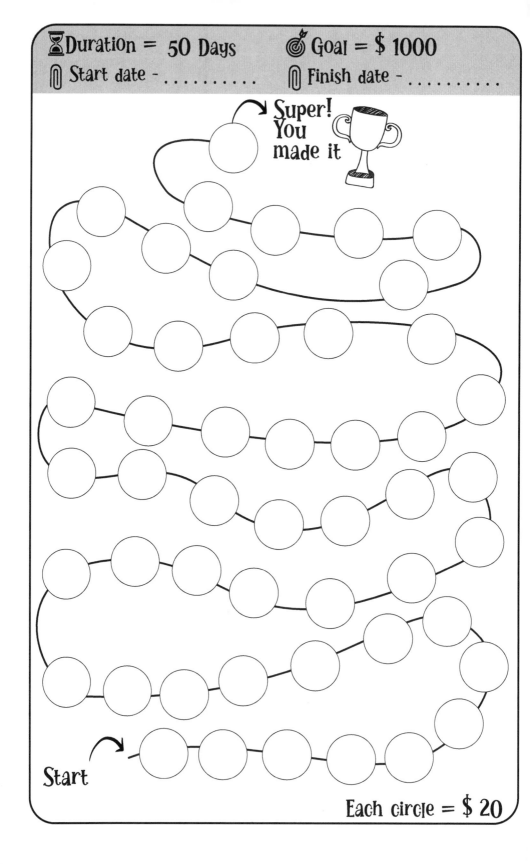

Duration = 50 Days   Goal = $ 1000

Start date - . . . .   Finish date - . . . .

Super! You made it

Start

Each circle = $ 20

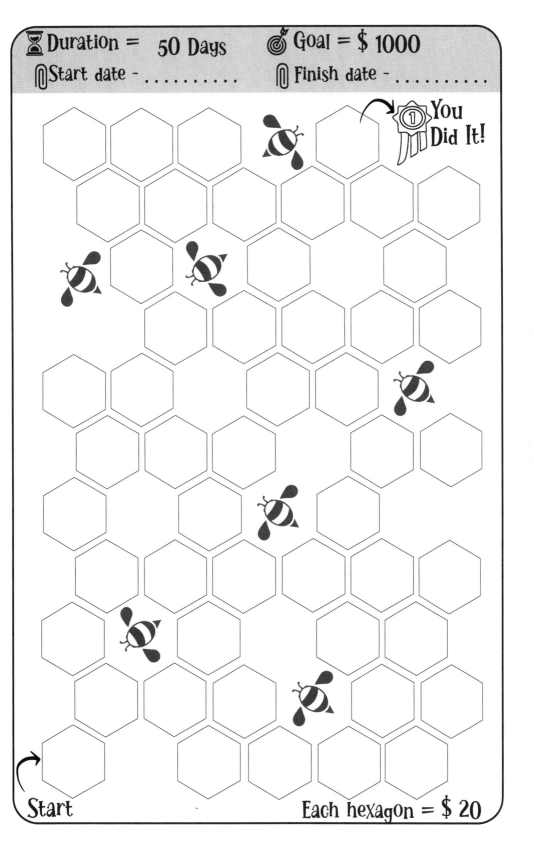

Duration = 50 Days   Goal = $ 1000

Start date - . . . .   Finish date - . . . .

You Did It!

Start   Each hexagon = $ 20

Awesome!
You Did It

Let's
Start
Here!

Let it
Bloom!

Each flower = $ 25

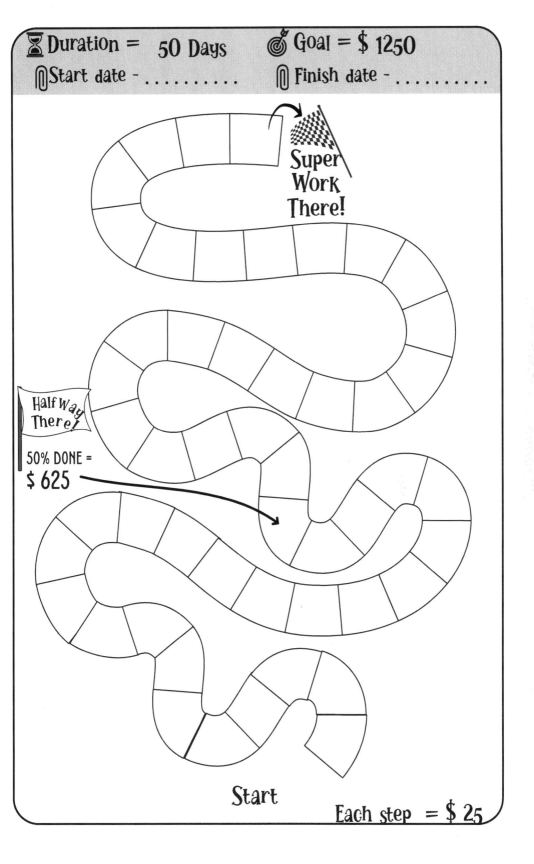

⏳ Duration = 50 Days   🎯 Goal = $ 1500
📎 Start date - . . . .   📎 Finish date - . . . .

Great!
You
made it

Start

Each heart= $ 30

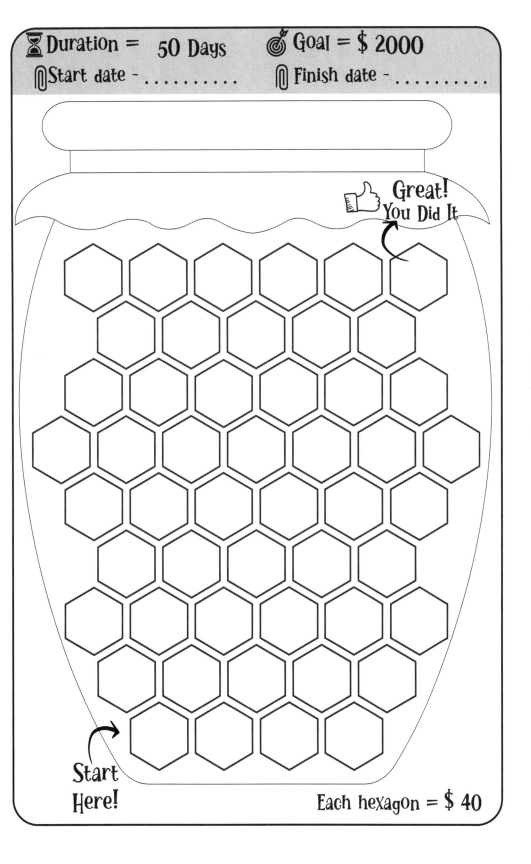

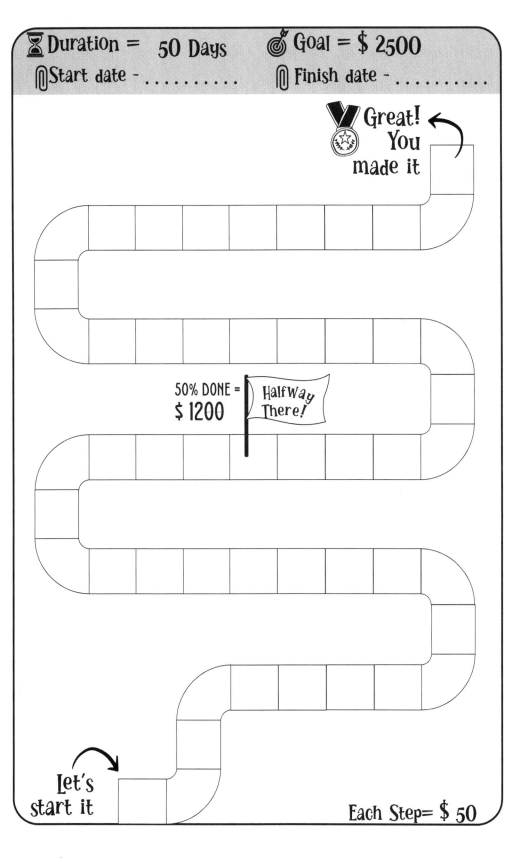

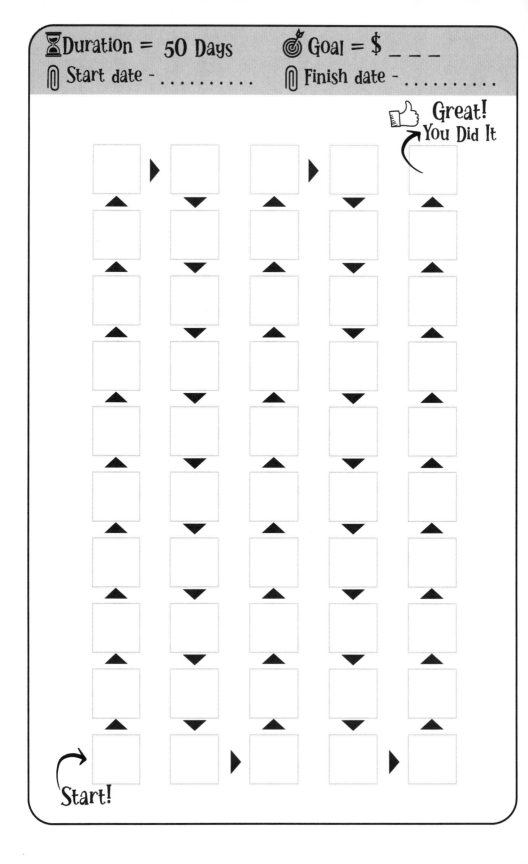

Duration = 50 Days   Goal = $ _ _ _
Start date - . . . .   Finish date - . . . .

Super!
You
made it

Start!

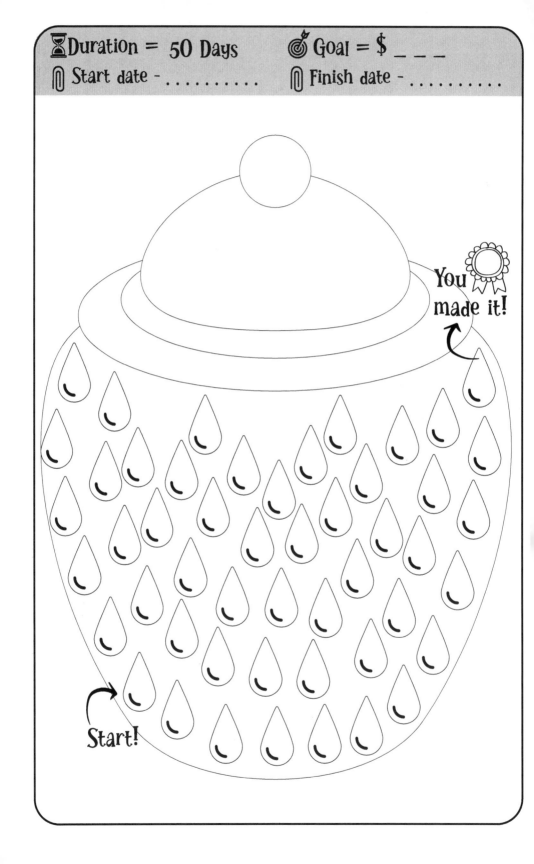

You made it!

Start!

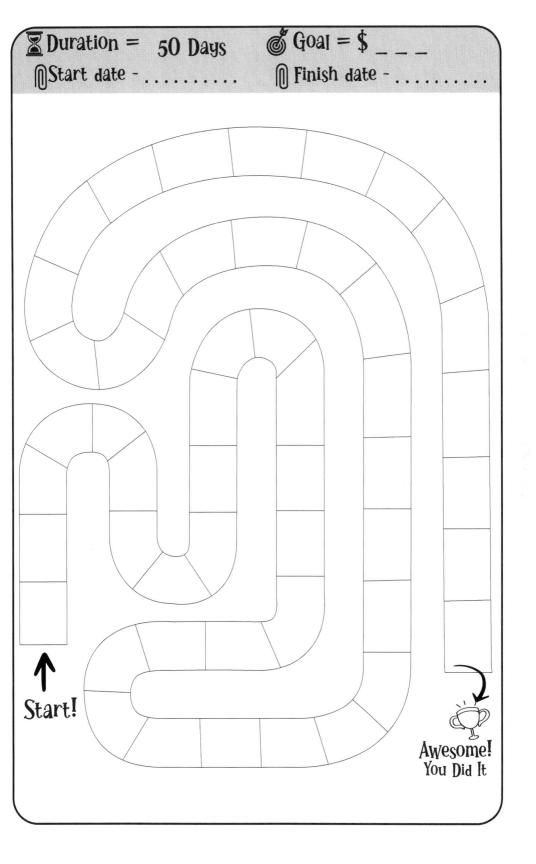

100 Days Money Saving Challenges

- ◘ $500 Saving Challenge - 2 Challenges
- ◘ $1000 Saving Challenge - 2 Challenges
- ◘ $5000 Savings Challenge - 2 Challenges
- ◘ Set your own challenge - 4 Challenges*

* Set your own challenge for 100 days
During this challenge you can save any amount or commit to any saving related activity. Depending on the challenge you decide to go forward, simply color in the icons accordingly.

Each challenge has a starting point and a finishing point. However, only in some challenges, you need to follow a specific path, and in others you can choose your own path to reach the finishing point. Once you start a challenge, keep going, do not break, and always try to finish within the given time period.

Per day/week saving amount is the same for some challenges and it is different for other challenges. So, depending on the challenge, choose the amount and save it for a particular week or day. Once you have that amount saved, simply color in the icon on each savings challenge and see your progress!

Happy Saving Journey !

100-Day
Savings
Challenges

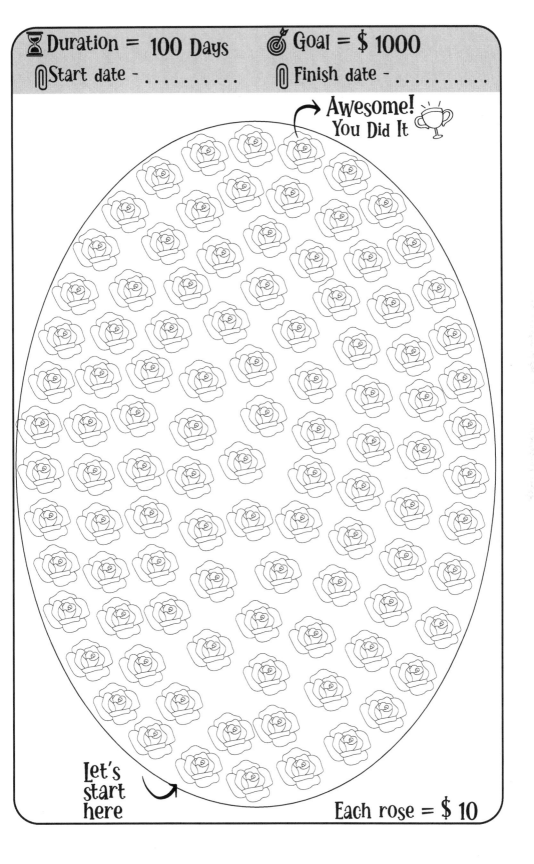

Awesome! You Did It 🏆

Let's start here

Each rose = $ 10

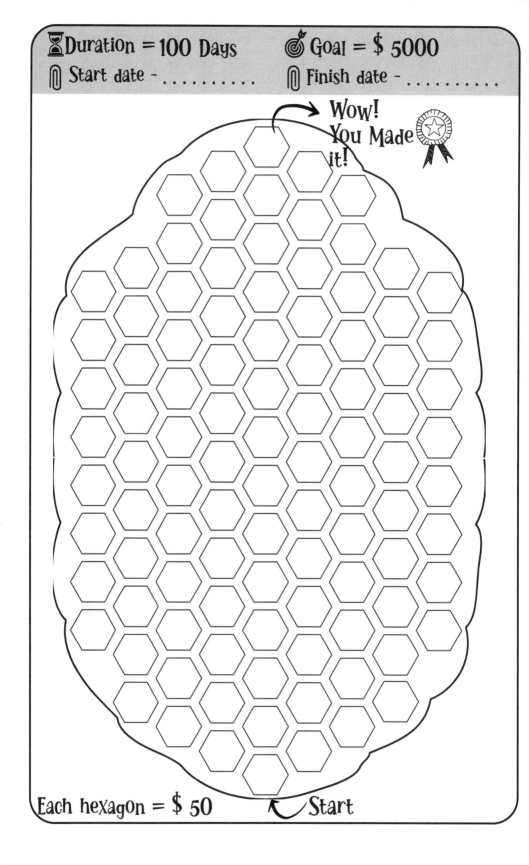

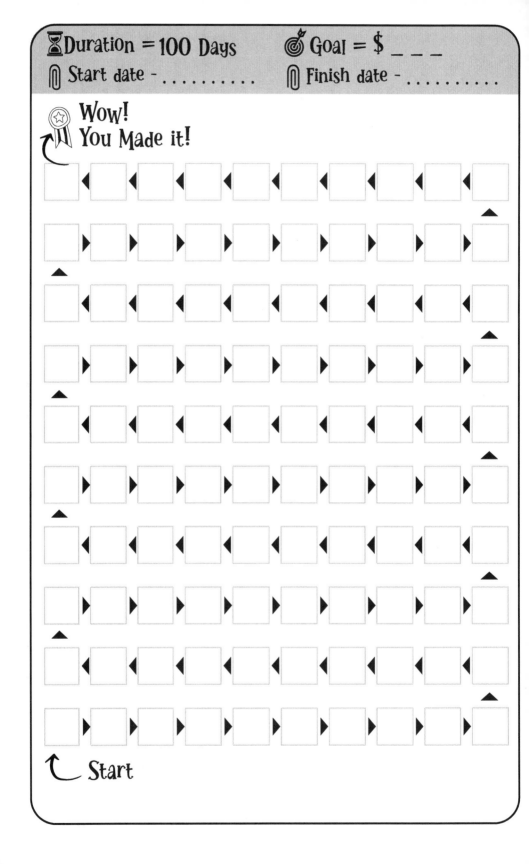

Duration = 100 Days   Goal = $ _ _ _

Start date - . . . .   Finish date - . . . .

Great!
You Did It

Start

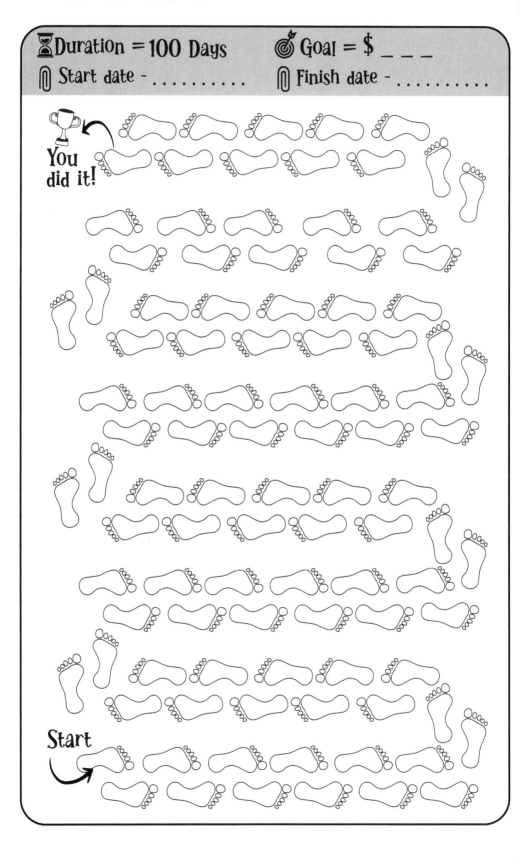

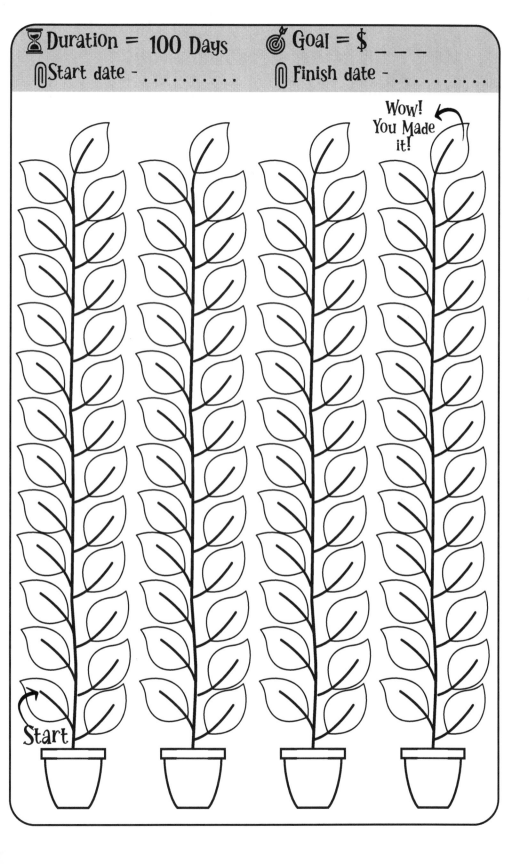

26 Week Money Saving Challenges

- ▫ +$ 1 Forward Saving Challenge (Save $351) - 2 Challenges
- ▫ -$ 1 Backward Saving Challenge (Save $351) - 2 Challenges
- ▫ +$ 2 Forward Savings Challenge (Save $702) - 2 Challenges
- ▫ -$ 2 Backward Savings Challenge (Save $702) - 2 Challenges
- ▫ $2000 Saving Challenge - 2 Challenges
- ▫ $2500 Savings Challenge - 2 Challenges
- ▫ $3000 Savings Challenge - 2 Challenges
- ▫ $5000 Savings Challenge - 2 Challenges
- ▫ $10000 Savings Challenge - 2 Challenges
- ▫ $15000 Savings Challenge - 2 Challenges
- ▫ Set your own challenge - 4 Challenges*

* Set your own challenge for 26 weeks
During this challenge you can save any amount or commit to any saving related activity. Depending on the challenge you decide to go forward, simply color in the icons accordingly.

Each challenge has a starting point and a finishing point. However, only in some challenges, you need to follow a specific path, and in others you can choose your own path to reach the finishing point. Once you start a challenge, keep going, do not break, and always try to finish within the given time period.

Per day/week saving amount is the same for some challenges and it is different for other challenges. So, depending on the challenge, choose the amount and save it for a particular week or day. Once you have that amount saved, simply color in the icon on each savings challenge and see your progress!
Happy Saving Journey !

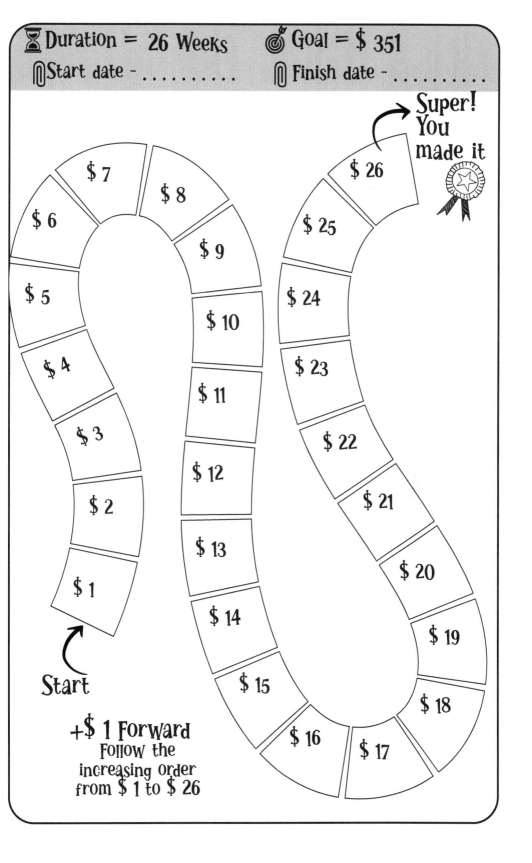

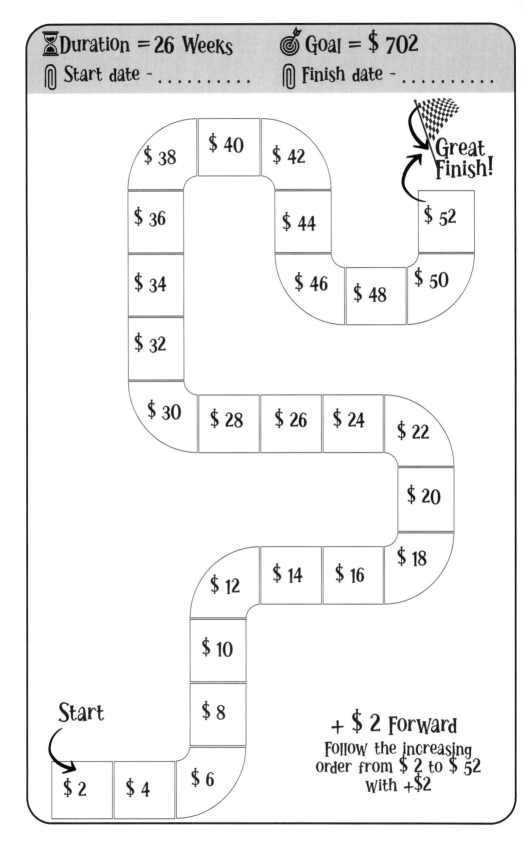

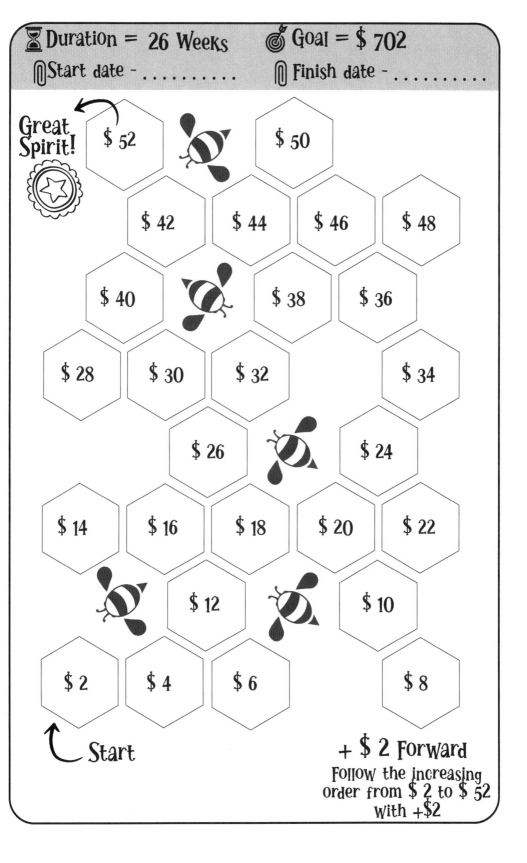

Duration = 26 Weeks   Goal = $ 702

Start date - . . . .   Finish date - . . . .

Great Work

$ 2 $ 4 $ 6 $ 8 $ 10

$ 16 $ 14 $ 12

$ 18 $ 20 $ 22 $ 24 $ 26

$ 36 $ 34 $ 32 $ 30 $ 28

$ 38 $ 40 $ 42

$ 52 $ 50 $ 48 $ 46 $ 44

Start

-$ 2 Reverse
Follow the decreasing
order from $ 52 to $ 2
with -$ 2

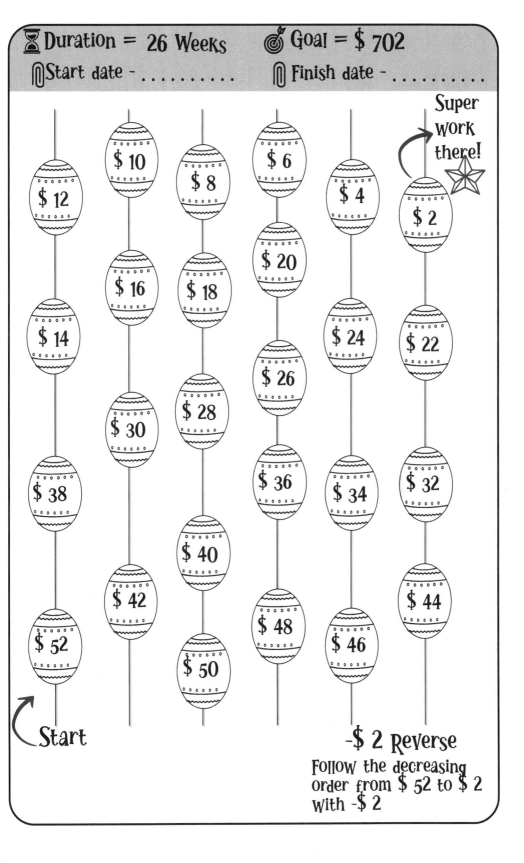

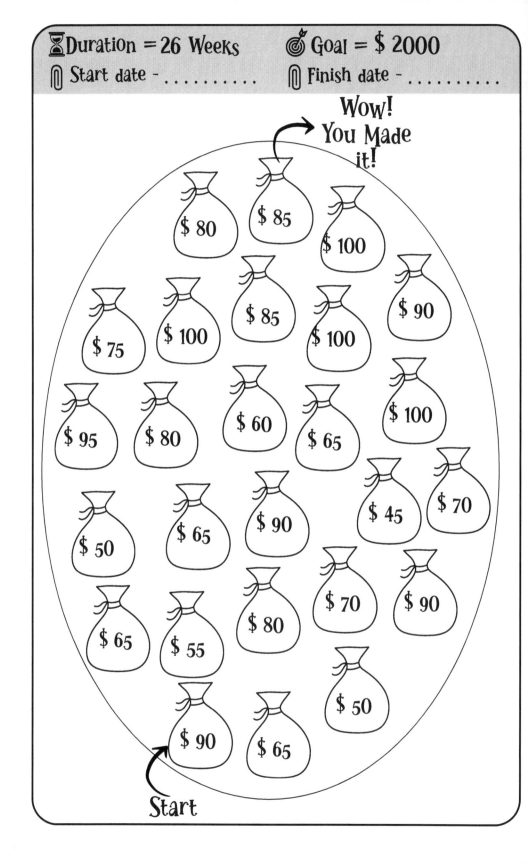

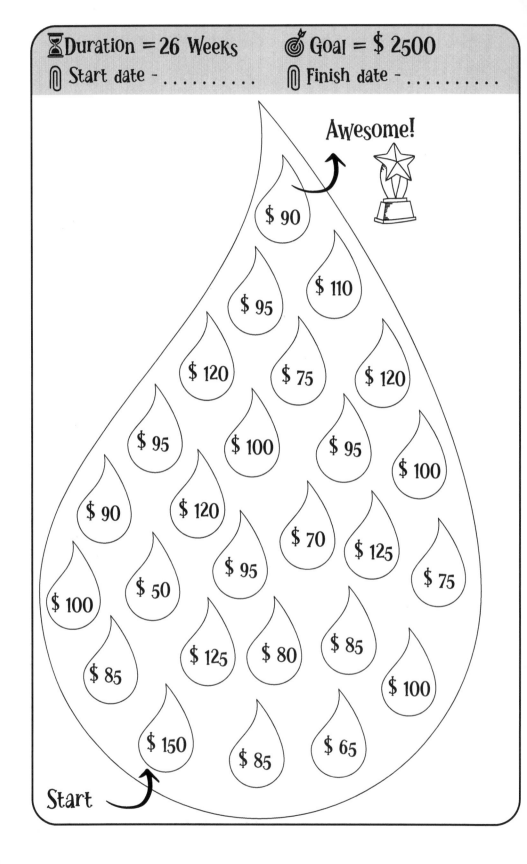

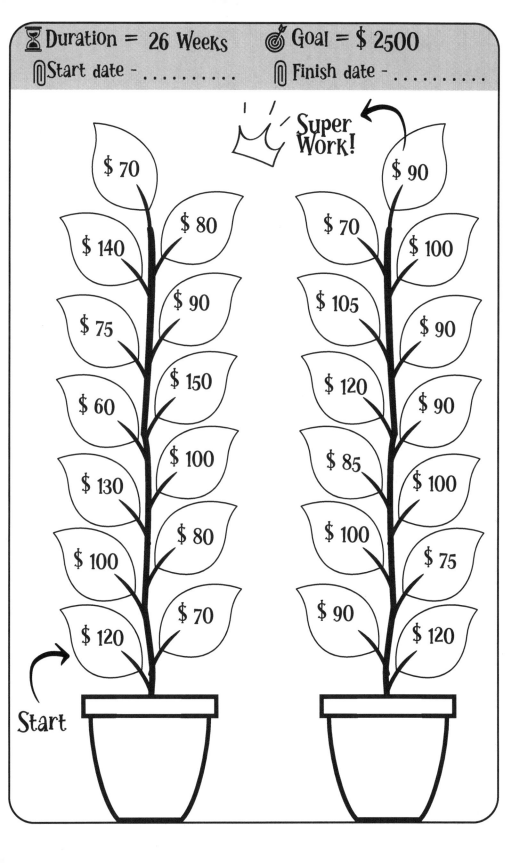

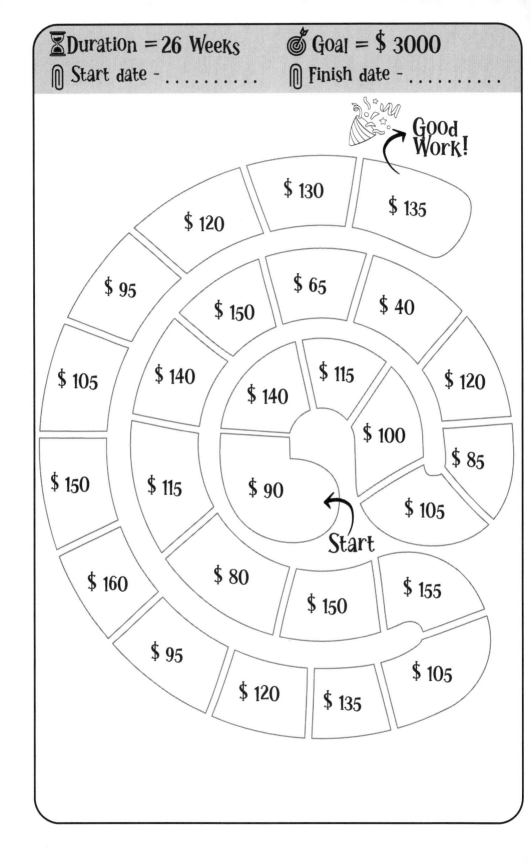

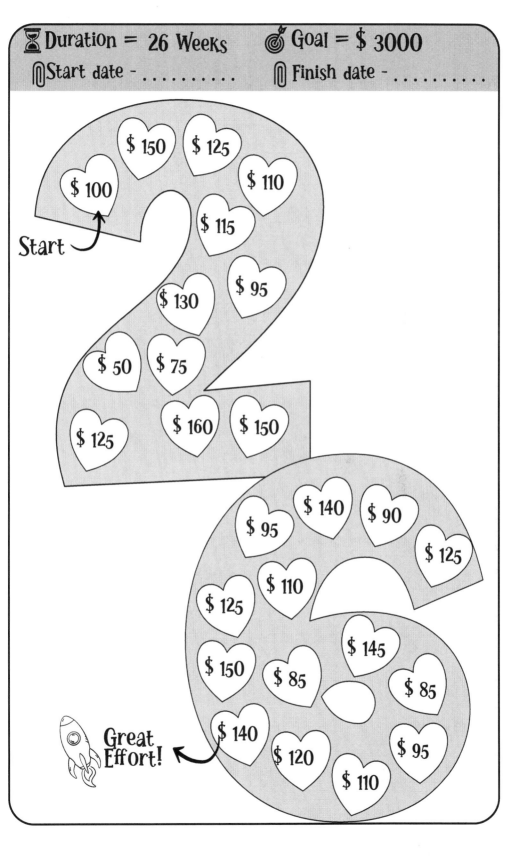

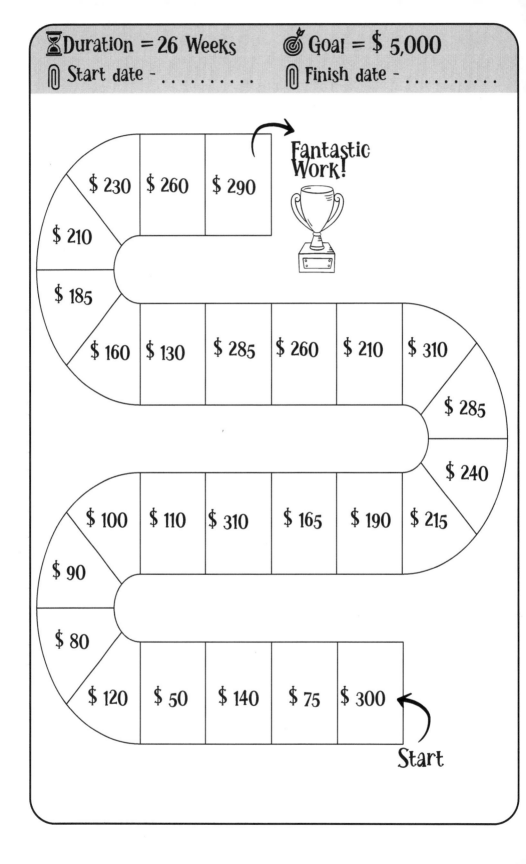

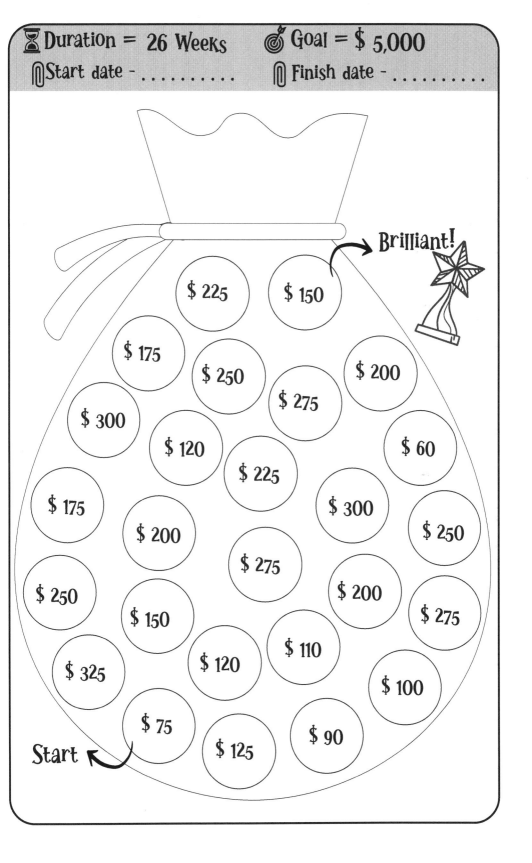

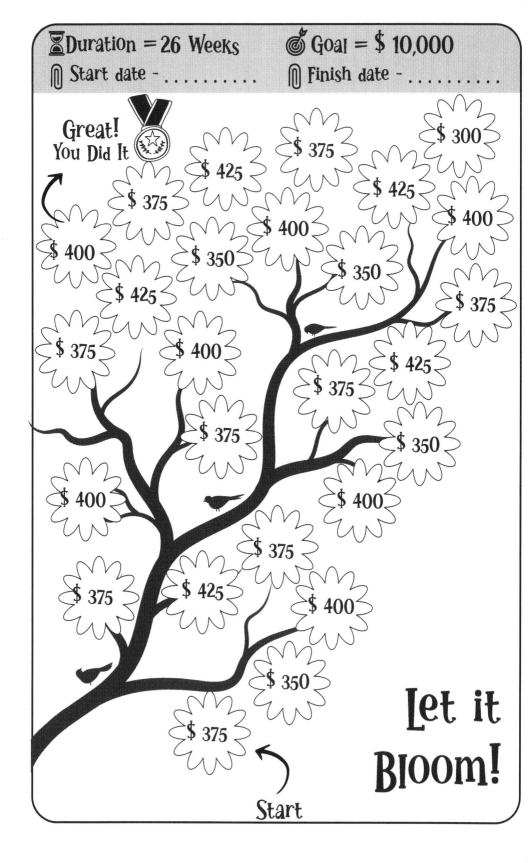

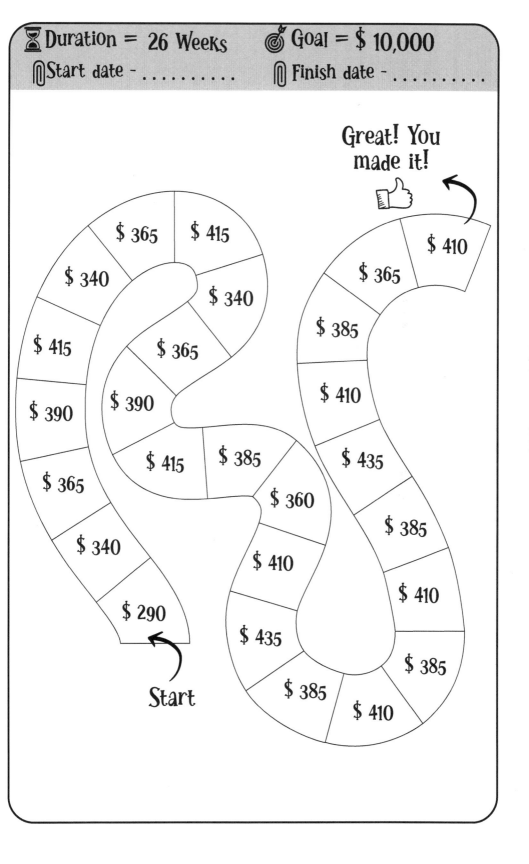

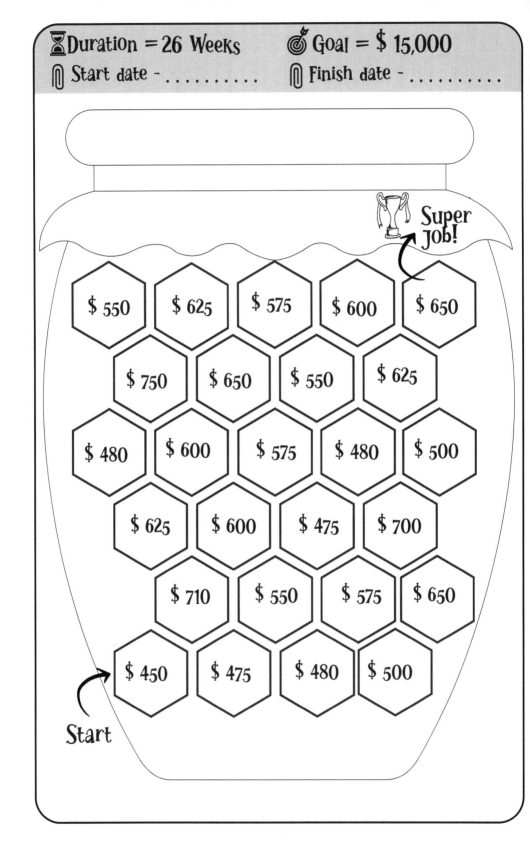

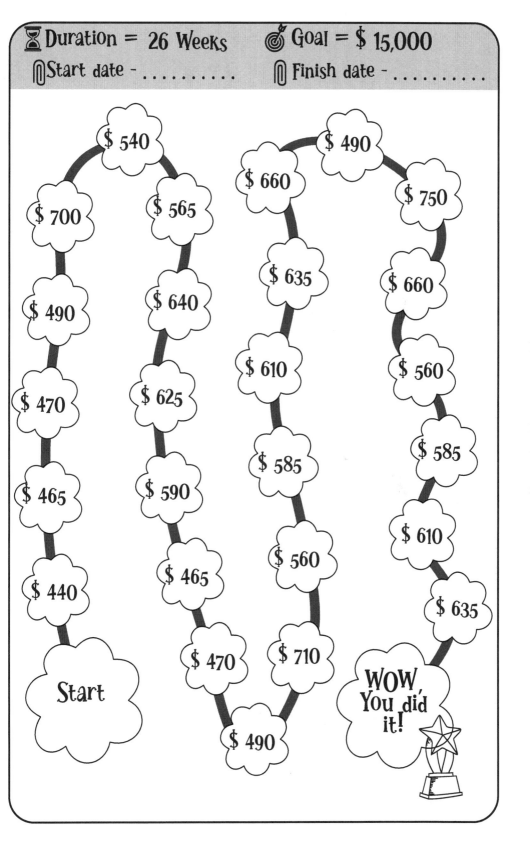

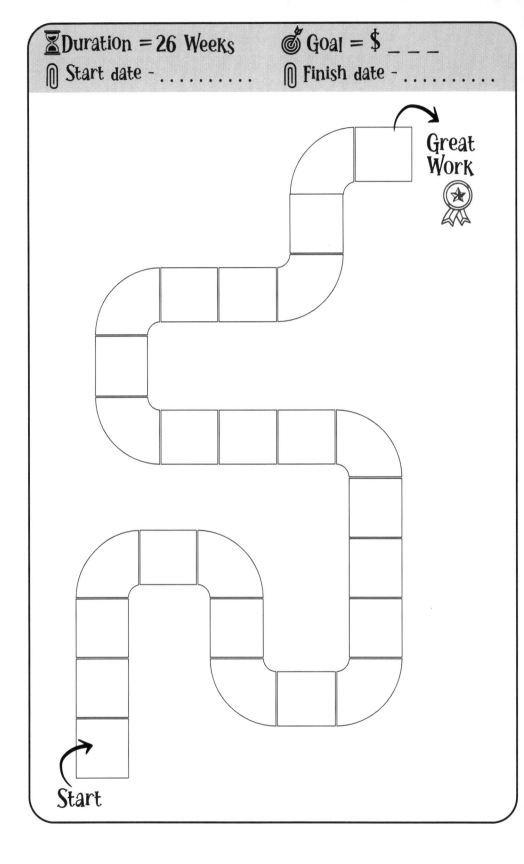

Awesome!

Start

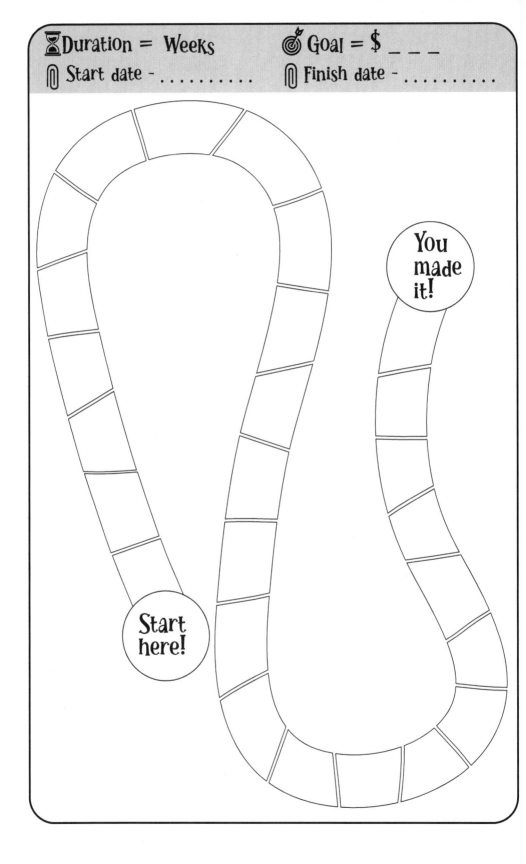

52 Week Money Saving Challenges

- +$ 1 Forward Saving Challenge (Save $ 1,378) - 2 Challenges
- -$ 1 Backward Saving Challenge (Save $ 1,378) - 2 Challenges
- +$ 2 Forward Savings Challenge (Save $2756) - 2 Challenges
- -$ 2 Backward Savings Challenge (Save $2756) - 2 Challenges
- $2000 Saving Challenge - 2 Challenges
- $2500 Savings Challenge - 2 Challenges
- $3000 Savings Challenge - 2 Challenges
- $5000 Savings Challenge - 2 Challenges
- $6000 Savings Challenge - 2 Challenges
- $10000 Savings Challenge - 2 Challenges
- $15000 Savings Challenge - 2 Challenges
- $20000 Savings Challenge - 2 Challenges
- Set your own challenge - 2 Challenges*

* Set your own challenge for 52 weeks
During this challenge you can save any amount or commit to any saving related activity. Depending on the challenge you decide to go forward, simply color in the icons accordingly.

Each challenge has a starting point and a finishing point. However, only in some challenges, you need to follow a specific path, and in others you can choose your own path to reach the finishing point. Once you start a challenge, keep going, do not break, and always try to finish within the given time period.

Per day/week saving amount is the same for some challenges and it is different for other challenges. So, depending on the challenge, choose the amount and save it for a particular week or day. Once you have that amount saved, simply color in the icon on each savings challenge and see your progress!

Happy Saving Journey !

52-Week Savings Challenges

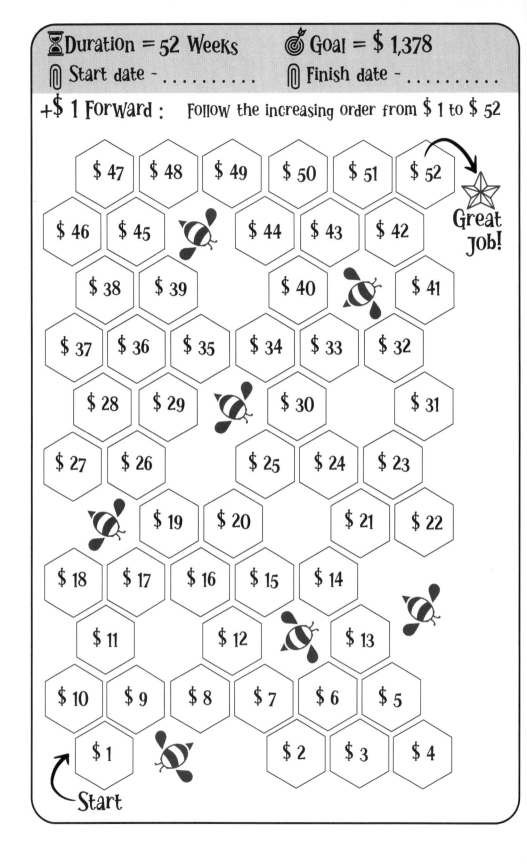

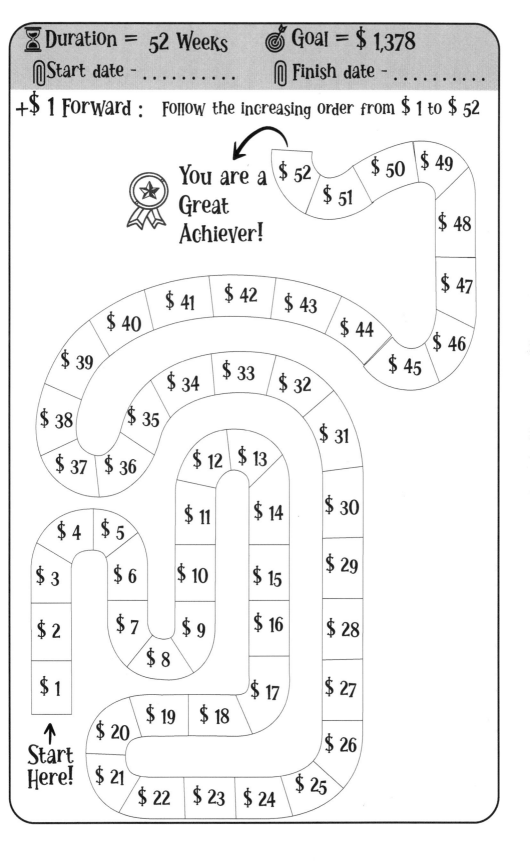

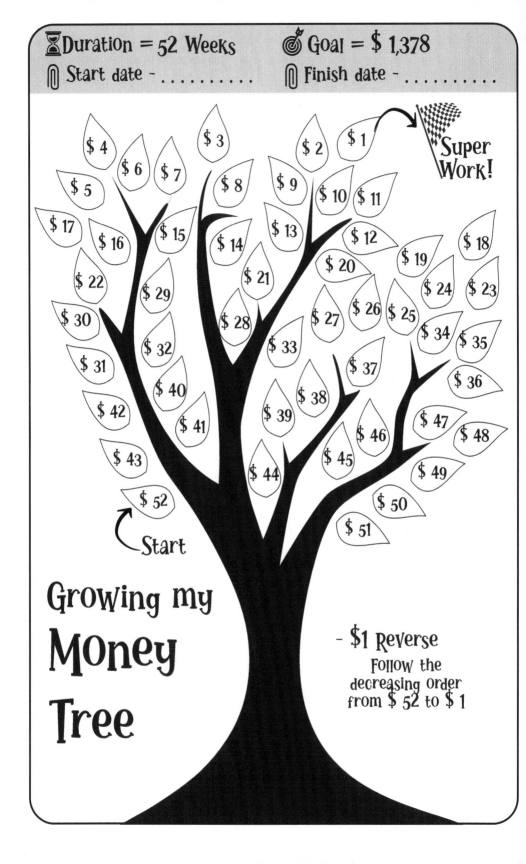

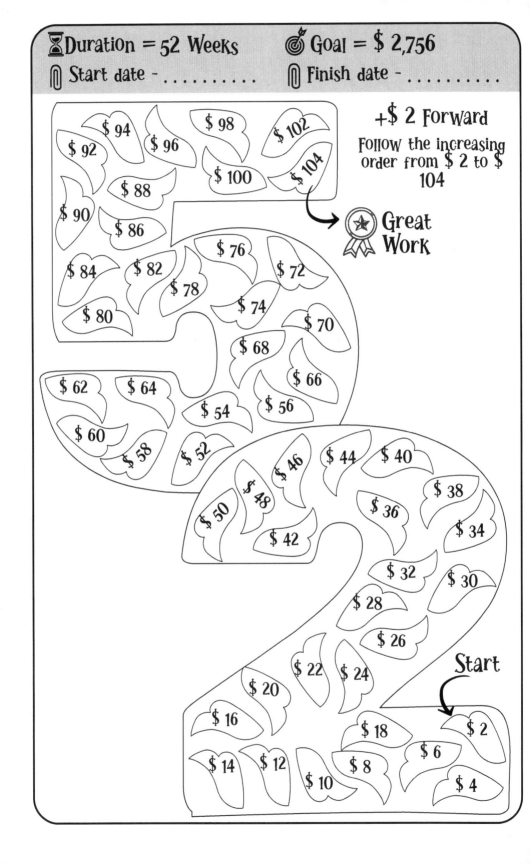

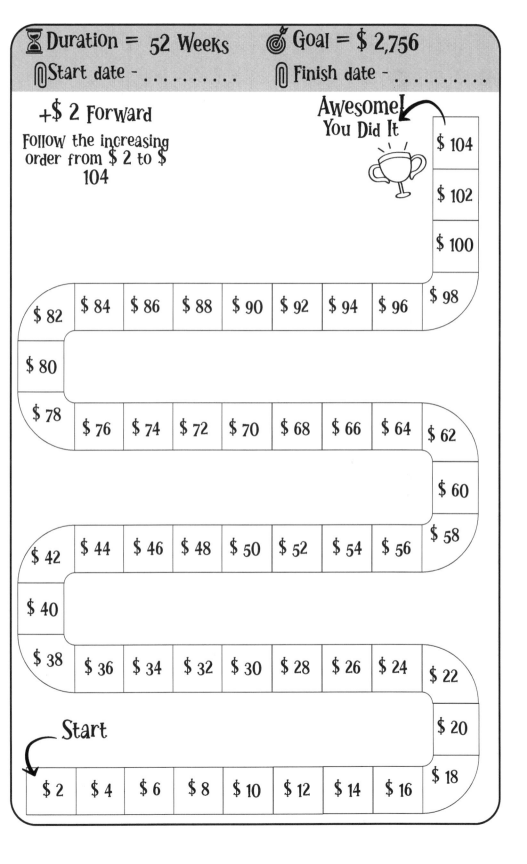

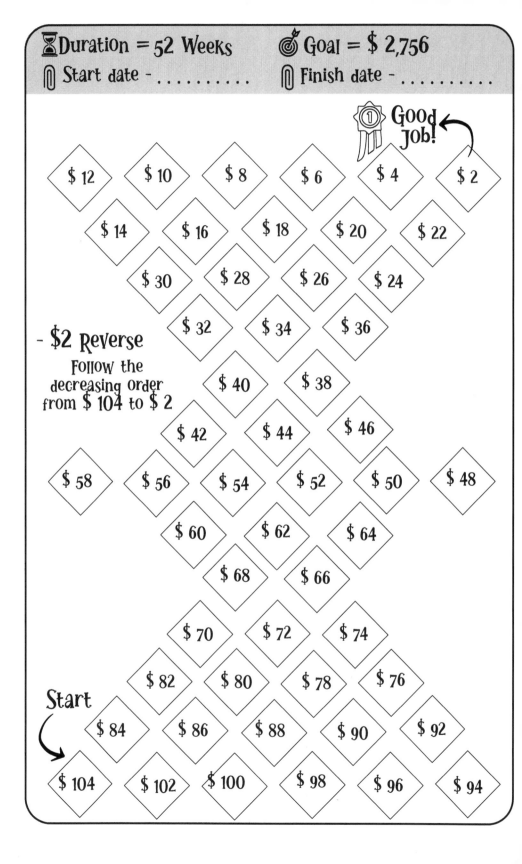

Duration = 52 Weeks   Goal = $ 2,756
Start date - . . . .   Finish date - . . . .

Good Job!

$ 12 $ 10 $ 8 $ 6 $ 4 $ 2

$ 14 $ 16 $ 18 $ 20 $ 22

$ 30 $ 28 $ 26 $ 24

$ 32 $ 34 $ 36

- $2 Reverse
Follow the decreasing order from $ 104 to $ 2

$ 40 $ 38

$ 42 $ 44 $ 46

$ 58 $ 56 $ 54 $ 52 $ 50 $ 48

$ 60 $ 62 $ 64

$ 68 $ 66

$ 70 $ 72 $ 74

$ 82 $ 80 $ 78 $ 76

Start

$ 84 $ 86 $ 88 $ 90 $ 92

$ 104 $ 102 $ 100 $ 98 $ 96 $ 94

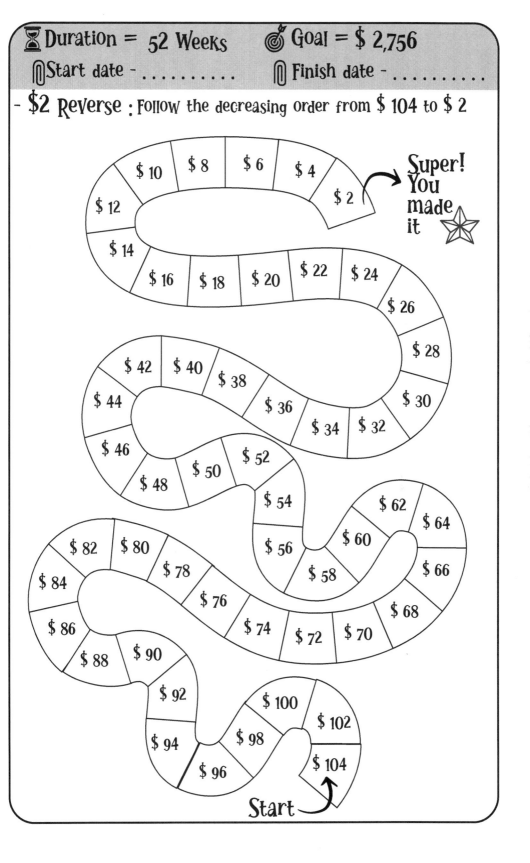

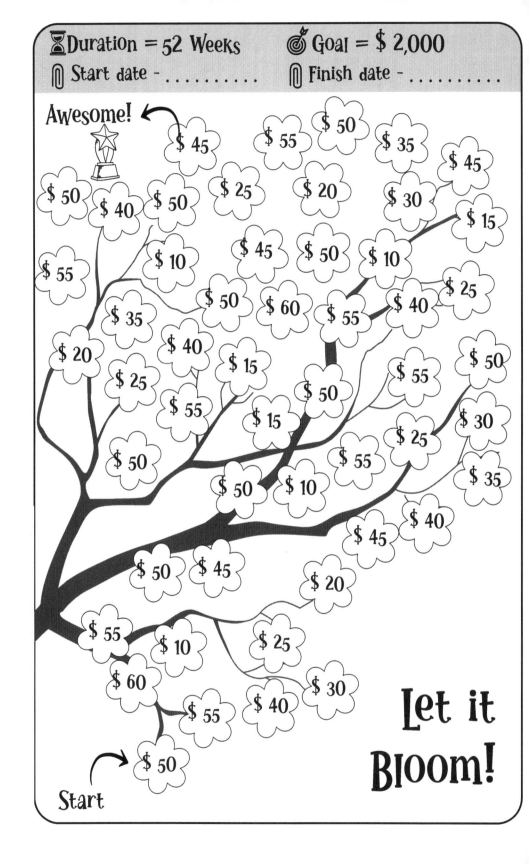

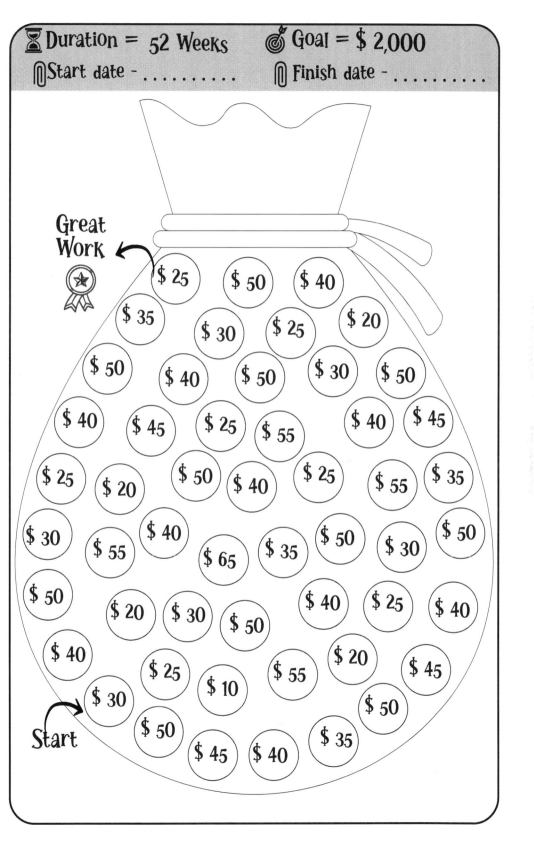

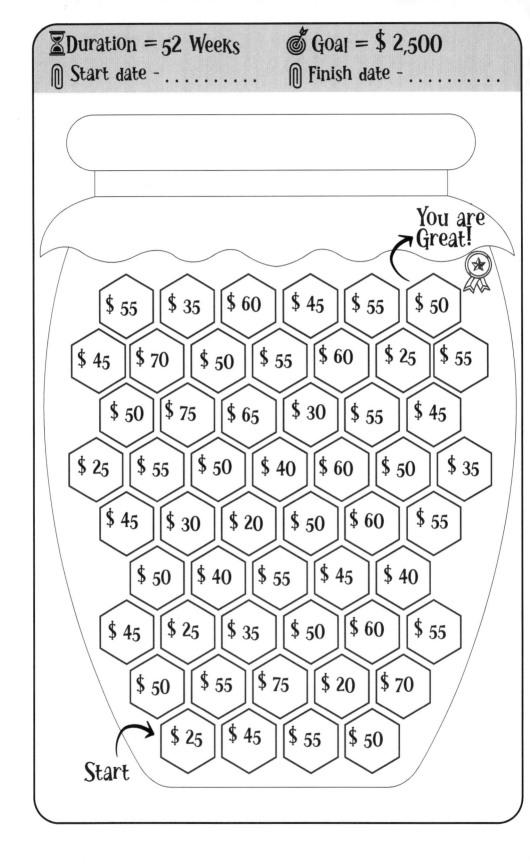

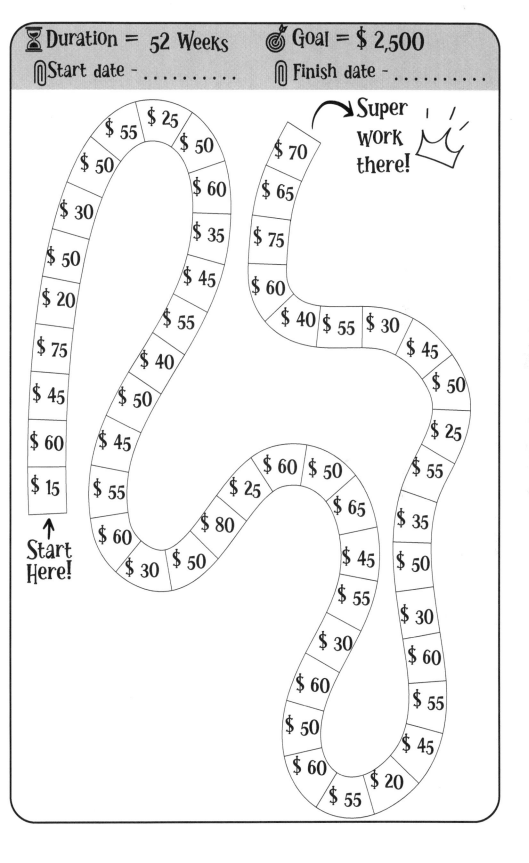

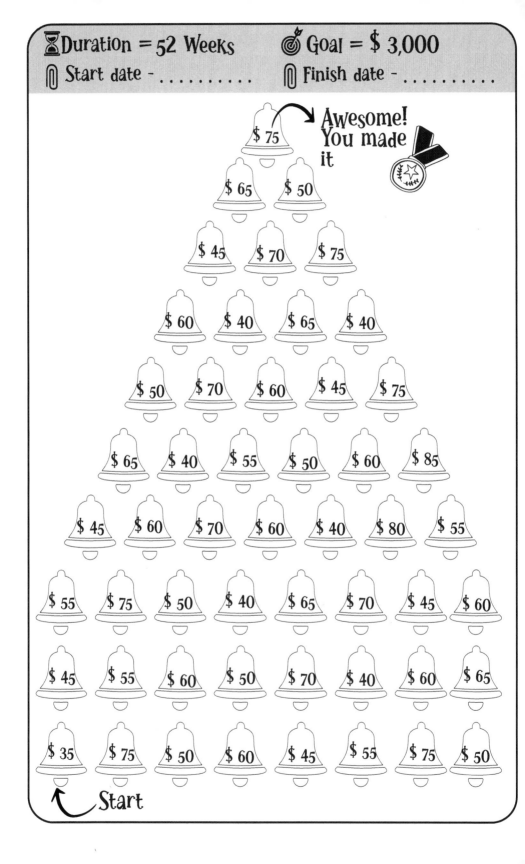

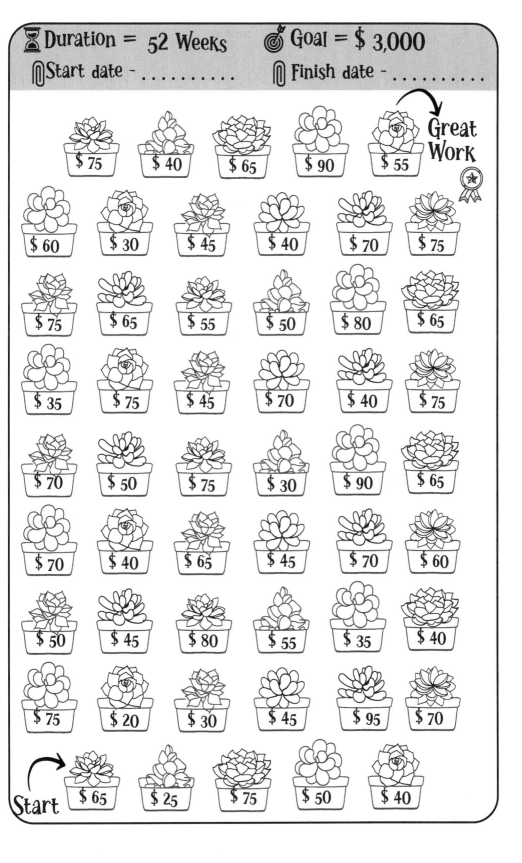

Duration = 52 Weeks   Goal = $ 3,000

Start date - . . . .   Finish date - . . . .

Great Work

$ 75 $ 40 $ 65 $ 90 $ 55

$ 60 $ 30 $ 45 $ 40 $ 70 $ 75

$ 75 $ 65 $ 55 $ 50 $ 80 $ 65

$ 35 $ 75 $ 45 $ 70 $ 40 $ 75

$ 70 $ 50 $ 75 $ 30 $ 90 $ 65

$ 70 $ 40 $ 65 $ 45 $ 70 $ 60

$ 50 $ 45 $ 80 $ 55 $ 35 $ 40

$ 75 $ 20 $ 30 $ 45 $ 95 $ 70

Start $ 65 $ 25 $ 75 $ 50 $ 40

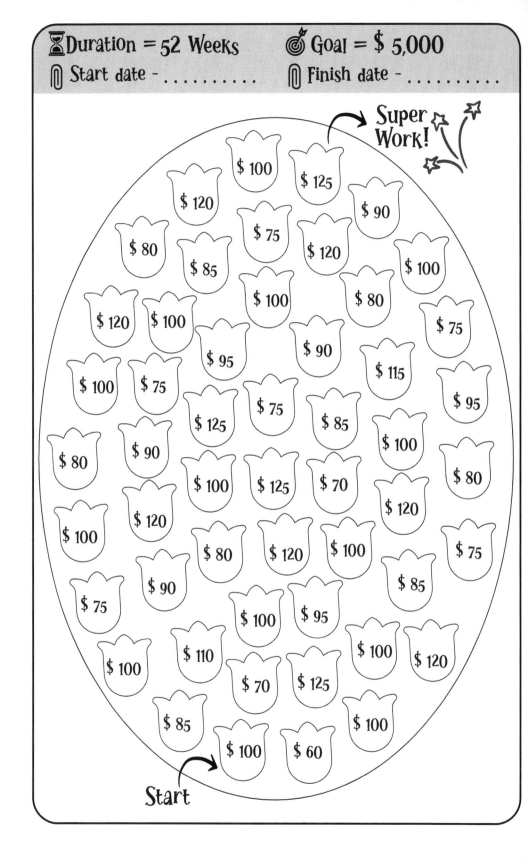

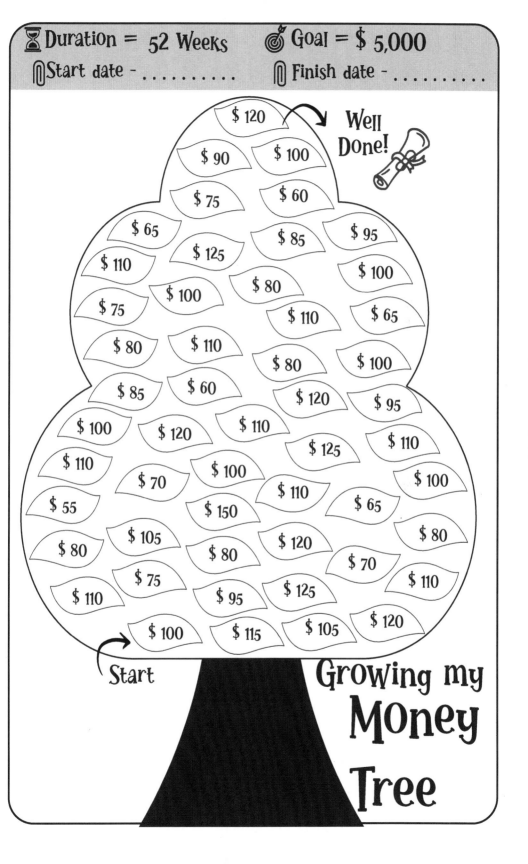

Duration = 52 Weeks   Goal = $ 6,000
Start date - . . . .   Finish date - . . . .

$ 100
$ 110 $ 90
$ 85 $ 115 $ 130
$ 105 $ 110
$ 130 $ 120 $ 150
$ 90 $ 140 $ 90 $ 85
$ 110 $ 135 $ 105
$ 65 $ 150
$ 100 $ 110 $ 130
$ 80 $ 130 $ 115 $ 110
$ 105 $ 155 $ 100
$ 125 $ 150 $ 120 $ 130
$ 130 $ 100 $ 155
$ 110 $ 110 $ 85 $ 90
$ 90 $ 155 $ 105
$ 130 $ 110
$ 105 $ 135 $ 130
$ 75 $ 160
$ 150

You are a
Great
Achiever!

Start

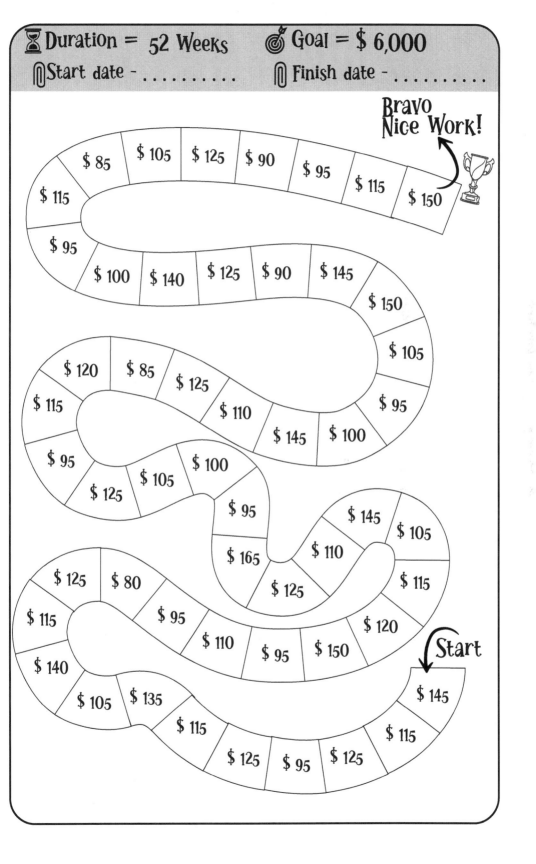

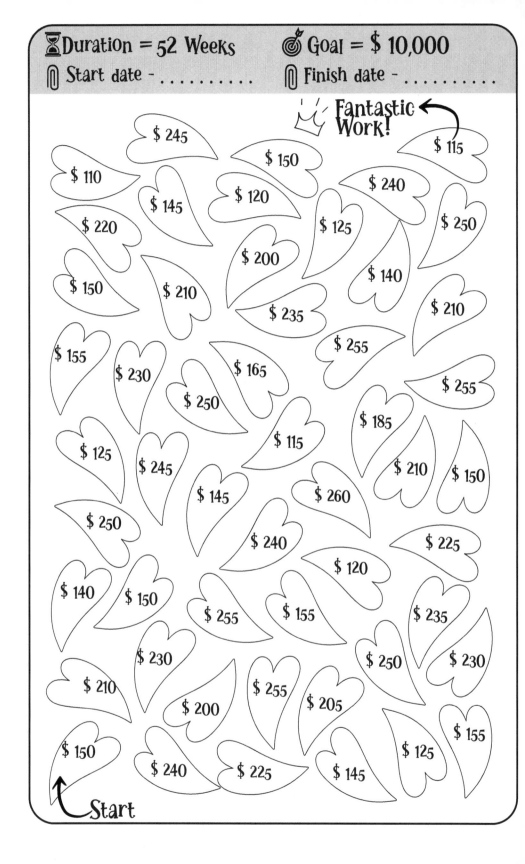

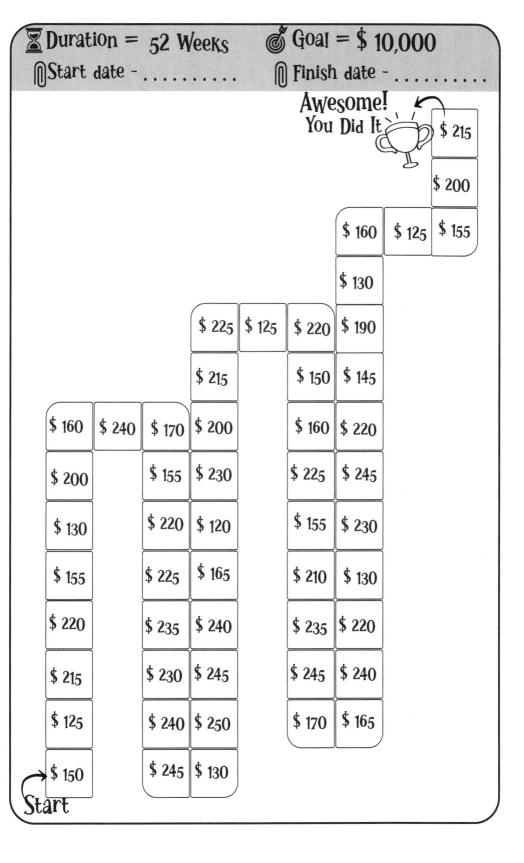

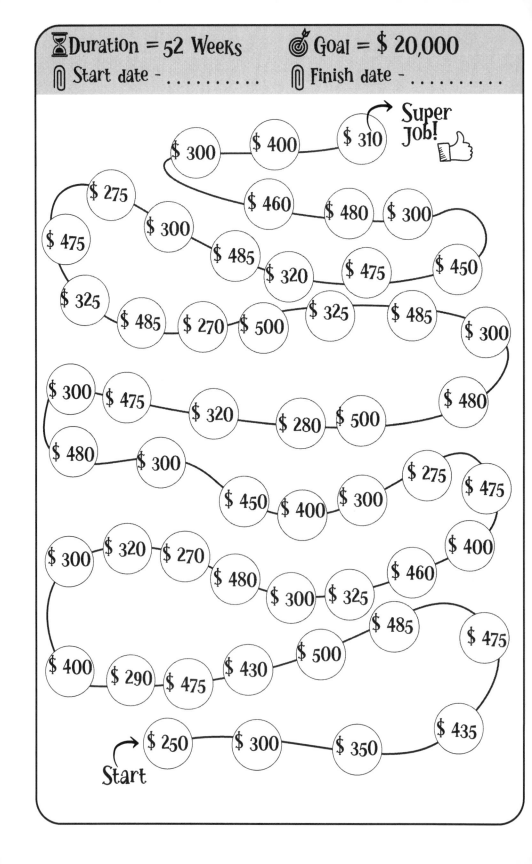

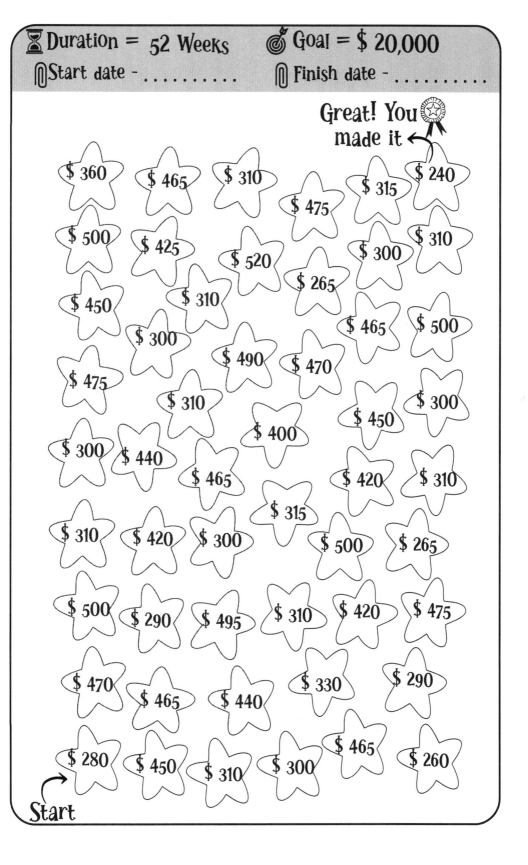

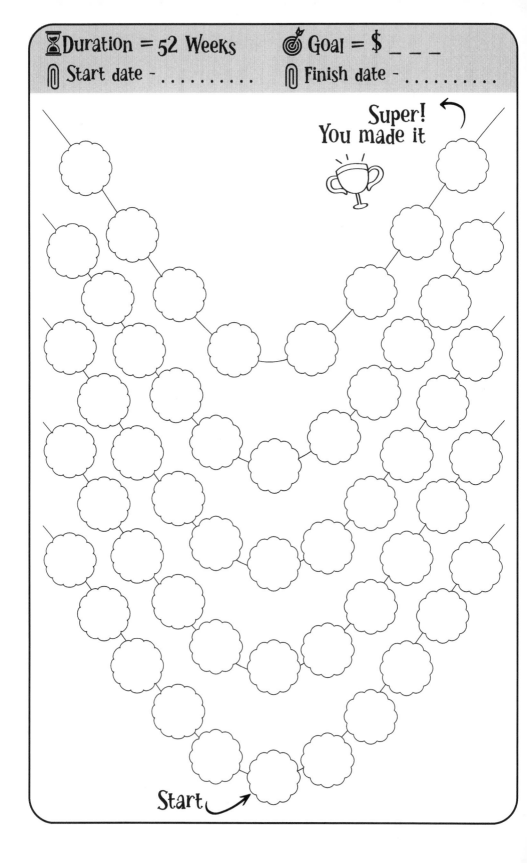

Thank you for this purchase from Aurora Publishing

Hope you enjoy this Awesome Savings Book of variety of Money Saving Challenges

Please let us know how you like it!

Positive ratings, reviews and constructive suggestions from awesome people like you help others to feel confident about choosing this book and help us to continue providing great books.

Share your happy experience online in Amazon with the following three steps;

★ Go to the product detail page of this book on **Amazon**

★ Scroll down to **Review** this product section

★ Click **Write a customer review** in the Customer Reviews section

★ Select a Star Rating

★ Scribble your happy thoughts, add photos and videos. Submit!

Thank you in advance for your review ♥

Aurora Publishing is passionate in designing and creating Logbooks, Record books, Journals with unique and effective designs to bring you that extra awesomeness you always wished for